SCARY PLACES

Ghastly Gothic Mansions

by Joyce Markovics

Consultant: Ursula Bielski
Author and Paranormal Researcher
Founder of Chicago Hauntings, Inc.

BEARPORT
PUBLISHING

New York, New York

Credits

Cover, © Ruth Black/Fotolia, © Franco Visintainer/Fotolia, © badahos/Fotolia, © Drobot Dean/ Fotolia, © ysbrandcosijn/Fotolia, and © Natalia Circova/Fotolia; 4–5, © khomlyak/Fotolia, © fsanchex/ Fotolia, © Ebgeniia Litovchenko/Shutterstock, and © Kim Jones; 6, Carol M. Highsmith/Public Domain; 6B, Alabama Department of Education/Public Domain; 7, © manx_in_the_world/iStock; 8, © Bidgee/CC BY-SA 4.0; 9, Public Domain; 10, © Gvanbriesen/CC BY-SA 3.0; 11T, © Everett Historical/Shutterstock; 11B, © Benjamin Dahlhoff/CC BY 3.0; 12, © Jeff Kerwin; 13T, © J. Helgason/Shutterstock; 13B, © Salvatore Di Vinti; 14, Derek Heidelberg/Public Domain; 15T, Public Domain; 15B, © Yuri Yakovlev/Dreamstime and © Olga Nikonova/Shutterstock; 16, Smallbones/Public Domain; 17T, © Toriwil/Flickr; 17B, © Everett Historical/Shutterstock; 18, © Oleg Bakhirev/Shutterstock; 19L, © MinervaStudio/Dreamstime; 19R, © Coffeemill/Shutterstock; 20, © Ron Cogswell; 21T, © Everett Historical/Shutterstock; 21B, © Everett Historical/Shutterstock; 22, © Google 2017; 23, © Kolbz/iStock; 24, © Doug Copeland; 25T, Public Domain; 25B, © PlusONE/Shutterstock; 26, © Baloncici/Shutterstock; 27, © Khaled El-fiqi/EPA/REX/ Shutterstock; 31, © hampusrw/Shutterstock.

Publisher: Kenn Goin
Senior Editor: Joyce Tavolacci
Creative Director: Spencer Brinker
Design: Dawn Beard Creative
Cover: Kim Jones
Photo Researcher: Thomas Persano

Library of Congress Cataloging-in-Publication Data

Names: Markovics, Joyce L., author.
Title: Ghastly Gothic mansions / by Joyce Markovics ; consultant, Ursula
   Bielski, author and paranormal researcher, founder of Chicago Hauntings, Inc.
Description: New York : Bearport Publishing Company, Inc., 2018. I Series:
   Scary places I Includes bibliographical references and index.
Identifiers: LCCN 2017007491 (print) I LCCN 2017021265 (ebook) I
ISBN 9781684023271 (ebook) I ISBN 9781684022731 (library)
Subjects: LCSH: Haunted houses—Juvenile literature. I
   Mansions—Miscellanea—Juvenile literature. I Ghosts—Juvenile literature.
Classification: LCC BF1475 (ebook) I LCC BF1475 .M28 2018 (print) I DDC
   133.1/2—dc23
LC record available at https://lccn.loc.gov/2017007491

For more information, write to Bearport Publishing Company, Inc., 45 West 21st Street, Suite 3B, New York, New York 10010. Printed in the United States of America.

10 9 8 7 6 5 4 3 2 1

Contents

Ghastly Gothic Mansions

Clouds hang low in a dark gray sky. The glowing moon peeks from behind a huge white house. The front door slowly creaks open, and a feeling of doom swells from inside. There's an ear-splitting *shriek*. Suddenly, an enormous mirror in the entranceway crashes to the ground, shattering into a thousand razor-sharp pieces. Reflected in each shard is the horror that has overtaken this ghastly **gothic** mansion.

In the 11 gothic mansions in this book, you will explore a house lit up by **phantom** fires, the **stately** site of a double murder, a cliffside castle where the ghost of a girl lingers, a home filled with human remains, and many other spooky sites.

Phantom Fires

The Drish House, Tuscaloosa, Alabama

For decades, the Drish House was left to rot. It became a crumbling shell of the elegant home it once was. Some believe that the **spirit** of the mansion's former owner dwells there—and that she sets the house ablaze every night.

The Drish House

John Drish and his wife, Sarah, began building their large house in 1837. It had a central tower, tall columns, and **ornate** plasterwork. John and Sarah lived happily in the mansion until one evening in 1867. According to one story, John began stumbling and acting strangely. Then he fell off the upstairs balcony to his death.

Sarah was overcome with grief. To busy herself, she spent all of her time planning John's **funeral**. Every detail had to be perfect, even the candles. After John was buried, Sarah never recovered and often thought about her own death. She became fixated on having the exact same funeral as her husband. The candles used at his funeral, she stated, must be reused at her own funeral. In 1884, Sarah drew her last breath. However, no one could find the candles from John's funeral, and Sarah's request was not carried out.

Not long after Sarah died, a passerby saw a fire burning in the mansion's tower. When firefighters arrived, there was no fire. The phantom fires still continue day after day. Some believe that Sarah's restless spirit is responsible for the ghostly blazes. Is she still upset about the lost candles and grieving for John?

Today, the Drish House is being restored to its former beauty. Yet what's to come of Sarah's restless spirit?

What the house looked like in 1911

7

Sinister Spirits

Monte Cristo Homestead, Junee, Australia

Built in 1885, this elegant Victorian house sits on a hill overlooking the town of Junee. Could it be the most haunted house in Australia? Olive Ryan, one of the owners, knew the answer to that question the moment she set foot on the property.

Monte Cristo Homestead

In 1963, Olive Ryan and her husband first arrived at their new house. Blinding light was shining from inside it, even though the electricity wasn't yet hooked up. This was the first of many spooky stirrings at Monte Cristo.

When Olive and her family began to look into the home's history, they grew even more unsettled. They discovered that a baby had died in the house. Supposedly, it had been yanked from the arms of a nanny by an unseen force and thrown down the stairs. Other stories tell of a boy who burned to death in the barn and a maid who jumped off the balcony to her death.

Olive has had countless terrifying experiences of her own. "I've had a hand on my shoulder," she said. "I've had my name called when I've been here by myself." She's also heard footsteps on the balcony where the maid is said to have jumped. Lawrence, Olive's son, has also had **eerie** encounters. "It always felt like someone was watching me." The Ryan family welcomes visitors to come see for themselves if the mansion really is spilling over with spirits.

The Ryans say they have also seen the Monte Cristo's long-dead original owners, Christopher and Elizabeth Crawley, in the house. White, shadowy figures thought to be the Crawleys also appear in photos taken inside the home.

Christopher and Elizabeth Crawley

Misery at Dusk

Boone Hall Plantation, Mt. Pleasant, South Carolina

Boone Hall is one of the oldest working **plantations** in the United States. Dating from 1681, the property includes a brickyard and nine small cabins that once housed hundreds of slaves. Sometimes, as the sun sets at Boone Hall, the horror that took place there long ago comes alive.

Boone Hall Plantation

At its peak, the plantation was home to 225 slaves. In addition to growing cotton and other crops, many of the enslaved people were forced to work at the property's brickyard. Making bricks was dangerous and backbreaking work. The slaves had to dig up clay from a nearby creek and then form it into bricks. To harden the bricks, the slaves baked them in a giant, fiery oven called a kiln. This was done at dusk when it was hard to see. As a result, accidents were all too frequent. Many of the enslaved workers were burned alive by the flames that poured out of the kiln.

Since that time, a ghost has been seen in the brickyard at dusk. She's hunched over and dressed in ragged clothes. She moves her hands in a repeated thrusting motion as though she's under a spell. Is the **apparition** a slave who lost her life in the brickyard's **inferno**?

Some visitors swear they've seen the ghosts of **Civil War** (1861–1865) soldiers **lurking** around Boone Hall. One ghostly soldier was spotted trying to remove a bullet from a fallen soldier's body.

A cabin on the estate where slaves once lived

"The Ghost Mansion"

Villa de Vecchi, Lake Como, Italy

Nestled in the mountains of Italy is Villa de Vecchi, or "The Ghost Mansion." Its empty windows look like soulless eyes. How did this once grand house become a dwelling for ghosts?

Villa de Vecchi

In the 1850s, a **nobleman** named Felix de Vecchi decided to build a summer home for his family near Lake Como. He hired Alessandro Sidoli to design and build a four-story mansion. The house included a stunning fountain, huge fireplaces, and a grand hall that held a piano. However, a year before it was finished, Alessandro passed away. It's thought his death may have set into motion a terrible curse.

Years later, it's said that Felix returned home one day to a scene of horror. He stumbled upon the dead body of his wife. Her face was badly **disfigured**. He also found that his beloved daughter had been kidnapped. For a long while, Felix searched for his child. Sadly, he never found her. Felix's sadness soon spiraled out of control. Unable to deal with the terrible losses, he took his own life in 1862. He was just 46 years old.

Today, people walking by the mansion often hear the eerie sound of a piano coming from inside the home's crumbling walls. Is it Felix's spirit tapping the keys?

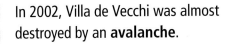

In 2002, Villa de Vecchi was almost destroyed by an **avalanche**.

13

Double Murder

Glensheen, Duluth, Minnesota

Many people insist that this 39-room **estate** isn't haunted. However, the piercing screams and glowing **orbs** might suggest otherwise. Could the fact that the house was the site of a double murder explain the eerie events?

Glensheen mansion was built in 1905.

When Elisabeth Congdon's father died, she **inherited** his fortune and Glensheen mansion. After raising her two children, Marjorie and Jennifer, Elisabeth enjoyed spending her final years at the mansion under the care of her nurse. Then **tragedy** struck. On June 27, 1977, a house worker spotted two legs dangling from a staircase landing. Then she saw the nurse's lifeless body in a pool of blood. A heavy brass candlestick lay nearby. The worker continued to Elisabeth's room. What she saw took her breath away. Elisabeth, too, was dead. She had been **smothered** with a satin pillow. Who could have carried out such an evil act?

Elisabeth Congdon

After her mother's death, Marjorie was to receive $8 million. Many people believe she wanted the money and would kill to get it. However, there wasn't any proof that Marjorie was guilty of the murders.

Today, visitors to Glensheen have been shaken by loud screams and moans at night. Others have seen ghostly orbs and clouds of mist that appear in the library where Elisabeth enjoyed reading.

Marjorie's husband went to jail for the murders. He later took his own life. Did Marjorie get away with murder?

Footsteps in the Night

Rockliffe Mansion, Hannibal, Missouri

Rockliffe Mansion is a 13,500-square-foot (1,254 sq m) home that was built on high, rocky ground above the city of Hannibal. Visitors to the house are transported back in time . . . and, perhaps, to a world in which spirits exist.

Rockliffe Mansion

A businessman named John J. Cruikshank built Rockliffe Mansion in the late 1890s. In 1924, John died in his bed. The house then sat empty for 43 years and fell into ruin.

In the 1960s, the city of Hannibal had plans to tear down Rockliffe. Just before the bulldozers arrived, townspeople found beautiful things, including antique lamps, rugs, art, and bedsheets inside the old house. The bedroom where John had died was untouched. A group of local residents decided to buy the mansion and **restore** it. At the time, they had no idea the house was a hangout for ghosts.

John J. Cruikshank's bedroom

On several occasions, caretakers have seen the **indentation** of a body in John's bed. People have repeatedly heard phantom footsteps. In fact, one night, one of the caretakers waited and listened as the ghostly footsteps grew louder. Then, when the footsteps finally reached her, she felt a rush of cool air blow past her face. Was it John's spirit making his nightly rounds?

The famous writer Mark Twain was raised in Hannibal and was a friend of John J. Cruikshank's. Twain visited Rockliffe Mansion frequently.

17

"The Green Lady"

Château de Brissac, Maine-et-Loire, France

Château de Brissac looks like a castle from a fairytale. However, if you look beyond its fancy **facade**, you will uncover a **sinister** story of betrayal and death.

Château
de Brissac

In the 1400s, Jacques de Brézé lived in Château de Brissac with his wife, Charlotte. Their marriage, however, was not a happy one. One day, Jacques found his wife with another man named Pierre de Lavergne. Jacques flew into a rage. On June 1, 1477, Charlotte and Pierre were found murdered! According to one story, Jacques plunged his sword into their bodies more than one hundred times. According to another story, Jacques strangled the lovers with his bare hands in a **chapel** in one of the castle's towers. No one knows for sure how they died, only that Charlotte and Pierre were never seen again.

Since the disappearances, a ghost that's believed to be Charlotte has been seen roaming the tower chapel. Early in the morning, her moans have been heard echoing through the castle. She appears to be wearing a flowing green gown, earning her the name "The Green Lady." What startles people most of all is her corpselike face. There are huge gaping holes where her eyes and nose should be.

Jacques de Brézé was arrested and jailed for the murders.

Ghostly Gallows

Perkins House, Charles Town, West Virginia

Covered in a tangle of ivy sits a red brick mansion dating from the 1800s. In the yard, there's an unusual carved stone beneath some trees. Most visitors would never guess that it marks the exact spot where the **abolitionist** John Brown dangled from a **gallows**.

Perkins House

JOHN BROWN SCAFFOLD
WITHIN THESE GROUNDS A
SHORT DISTANCE EAST OF
THIS MARKER IS THE SITE OF
THE SCAFFOLD ON WHICH
JOHN BROWN, LEADER OF
THE HARPERS FERRY RAID,
WAS EXECUTED DECEMBER
THE SECOND, 1859.
ERECTED BY THE JEFFERSON COUNTY
HISTORICAL SOCIETY OF WEST VIRGINIA 1972

Born in Connecticut in 1800, John Brown believed that slavery was a horrible crime. For many years, he worked to peacefully put an end to it. However, despite his efforts, little changed in the United Sates. He believed more needed to be done—even if it meant taking **violent** action. On October 16, 1859, in Harpers Ferry, West Virginia, John planned a slave uprising. He and a group of 21 men stole weapons from a U.S. **arsenal**. John was hoping that thousands of slaves would fight alongside him—but they never came. Although John and his men fought fiercely, they were no match for U.S. Colonel Robert E. Lee and his men. Two days later, John was captured and thrown in prison.

John Brown

Weeks later, John was convicted of **treason** and sentenced to death. Before he died, John said he was glad to give up his life for the millions of slaves without rights. "So let it be done!" he shouted. On December 2, 1859, John Brown was hanged where the Perkins House now stands. Since that time, it's said that John's ghost walks the property ready to fight for the cause he cared so deeply about.

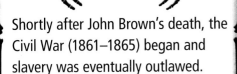

Shortly after John Brown's death, the Civil War (1861–1865) began and slavery was eventually outlawed.

The fiery John Brown at the gallows

A Blind Leap

Castelinho de São João, Estoril, Portugal

Castelinho de São João was built to look like a small castle. It sits on a steep cliff overlooking the Atlantic Ocean. Long ago, as the ocean waves crashed against the cliff, they drowned out the screams of a young girl who fell to her death.

Castelinho de São João

In the 1980s, a man named José Castelo Branco was looking for a beautiful seaside property to buy. He thought he had found it in Castelinho de São João. Little did he know that the castle literally had views to die for.

The day José went to see the castle was sunny and beautiful. He decided to go for a walk along the cliff at the edge of the property. As he strolled in the warm sunshine, he saw a little girl on the narrow pathway. She stood still without saying a word. Her eyes seemed to pierce through his body. Suddenly, José felt a strange pull. Something inside him was telling him to move closer to the cliff's edge. Then the urge to throw himself into the sea overtook him. He fought the **impulse** and immediately left the property. Who was that girl, and what had José just experienced?

After looking into the history of the house, José discovered that an awful accident had occurred there. In the 1700s, a young blind girl was walking along the cliff when she fell to her death. Chills raced down José's spine. He suddenly realized he had met the young girl's ghost!

Other visitors to Castelinho de São João have also claimed to experience the strange desire to jump off the cliff.

Death and More Death

Franklin Castle, Cleveland, Ohio

Whirling lights, chilling cries, doors flying off their hinges—these are just some of the strange things visitors have reported at Franklin Castle. Could the ghostly events have anything to do with the mansion's mysterious past?

Franklin Castle is also known as the Tiedemann House.

Hannes Tiedemann built Franklin Castle in 1881 for his wife, children, and mother. The stone mansion is topped with towers and **gargoyles**, giving it a castle-like appearance. It has more than 20 rooms, including a huge ballroom, and, some believe, several secret passageways.

Hannes Tiedemann

Not long after it was built, a string of mysterious deaths took place at the castle. In 1891, Hannes's mother and young daughter died within weeks of each other. During the next three years, Hannes and his wife buried three more children. The youngest child was just 11 days old. The cause of the childrens' deaths is unknown. When Hannes's wife passed away in 1895, neighbors began to wonder whether Hannes was involved in the deaths.

By 1908, the entire Tiedemann family, including Hannes, had died. When the bones of children were discovered in a cabinet in the house, people began to believe the rumors that Hannes was a murderer. Or is there another explanation for all the deaths?

According to a legend, Hannes might have also killed his young niece by hanging her from a beam in a secret room in the castle.

A Dark Dream

Baron Empain Palace, Cairo, Egypt

Rising out of the Egyptian desert near Cairo is a sand-colored palace. The majestic house **lures** visitors in for a closer look. However, guests should beware. This old palace holds secrets that are better left in the dark.

Baron Empain Palace

Édouard Louis Joseph Empain, better known as Baron Empain, made millions of dollars building railroads in Europe. In 1904, he went on a trip to Egypt and fell in love with the country. He bought a large piece of land outside Cairo on which to build a grand home for his wife and daughter. In 1907, he began building a palace inspired by ancient **temples** in Cambodia. The main feature of the house was a huge tower that contained a spiral staircase. It's believed the staircase was built on a giant platform that spun all the way around.

Édouard's dream of a perfect house soon became a nightmare. One day, his wife tumbled down the spinning staircase and died. His **distressed** daughter then hid away in the dark basement. A few years later, she, too, was found dead in the palace.

The spiral stairs, known as the Staircase of Death

Today, the empty palace is home to thousands of bats and—some say—ghosts. Shadowy spirits have been seen wandering through the house. Their ghostly voices can be heard as the bats take flight into the night sky.

In 1929, Baron Empain died. At the time of his death, it's said that mirrors in the palace dripped with blood.

Ghastly Gothic Mansions

Glensheen
Duluth, Minnesota

Spirits linger at this bloody site of a double murder.

Franklin Castle
Cleveland, Ohio

What else is hidden away in this mansion with an evil past?

Perkins House
Charles Town, West Virginia

Visit the property where a famous abolitionist drew his last breath.

NORTH AMERICA

Rockliffe Mansion
Hannibal, Missouri

There's something sinister at this rundown mansion.

Boone Hall Plantation
Mt. Pleasant, South Carolina

A horrible past comes to light at this spooky site.

The Drish House
Tuscaloosa, Alabama

Visit a mansion where a spirit sets phantom fires.

SOUTH AMERICA

Atlantic Ocean

Pacific Ocean

N

W E

S

Around the World

Château de Brissac
Maine-et-Loire, France

Make way for the Green Lady ghost. She has a bone to pick.

EUROPE

ASIA

Villa de Vecchi
Lake Como, Italy

How did this once grand house become a dwelling for ghosts?

Baron Empain Palace
Cairo, Egypt

Beautiful palace or house of horror? This old house holds countless secrets.

Arctic
Ocean

AFRICA

Castelinho de São João
Estoril, Portugal

Watch your step at this spooky cliffside castle.

Indian
Ocean

AUSTRALIA

Monte Cristo Homestead
Junee, Australia

Could this be the most haunted house in Australia?

Southern
Ocean

ANTARCTICA

Glossary

abolitionist (ab-*uh*-LISH-uh-nist) someone who opposes slavery

apparition (*ap*-uh-RISH-uhn) a ghost or ghostlike image

arsenal (AHR-suh-nuhl) a place where guns and military equipment is stored

avalanche (AV-uh-lanch) a large amount of snow, ice, or rock that suddenly moves down a mountain

chapel (CHAP-uhl) a small church

Civil War (SIV-il WOR) the U.S. war (1861–1865) between the southern and northern states

disfigured (dis-FIG-yurd) changed or ruined by injury or some other cause

distressed (diss-TRESSD) troubled

eerie (EER-ee) mysterious, strange

estate (i-STAYT) a big house on land

facade (*fuh*-SAHD) the front of a building

funeral (FYOO-nuh-ruhl) a ceremony that's held after a person dies

gallows (GAL-ohz) a wooden structure used to hang criminals

gargoyles (GAHR-goilz) carved figures of strange-looking humans or animals

gothic (GOTH-ik) gloomy or mysterious

impulse (IM-puhls) a sudden drive to do something

indentation (in-den-TEY-shuhn) a deep cut or pit in something

inferno (in-FUR-noh) a large fire or a place that's like hell

inherited (in-HERR-uh-tid) received something, such as money, from someone who has died

lures (LOORS) to attract something

lurking (LURK-ing) secretly hiding

nobleman (NOH-buhl-muhn) someone who has a high social status

orbs (AWRBS) glowing spheres

ornate (awr-NAYT) elaborately decorated

phantom (FAN-tuhm) ghostly

plantations (plan-TAY-shuhnz) large farms where crops are grown

restore (ri-STOR) to bring something back to its original condition

sinister (SIN-*uh*-stur) dark or evil

smothered (SMUTH-urd) killed someone by covering the nose and mouth so he or she can't breathe

spirit (SPIHR-it) a supernatural being, such as a ghost

stately (STEYT-lee) majestic

temples (TEM-puhlz) religious buildings where people go to pray

tragedy (TRAJ-uh-dee) a sad and terrible event

treason (TREE-zuhn) the act of overthrowing the government

violent (VAHY-uh-luhnt) acting with uncontrolled force

Bibliography

Austin, Joanne. *Weird Hauntings: True Tales of Ghostly Places.* New York: Sterling (2006).

Mills, Roger P. *Haunted: Houses, Mansions, & Estates of America You'd Never Enter: Behind Their Creepy Doors.* New York: CreateSpace (2017).

Read More

Hamilton, John. *Haunted Places (The World of Horror).* North Mankato, MN: ABDO (2007).

Markovics, Joyce. *Haunted Gotham (Scary Places).* New York: Bearport (2017).

Williams, Dinah. *Dark Mansions (Scary Places).* New York: Bearport (2012).

Learn More Online

To learn more about ghastly gothic mansions, visit
www.bearportpublishing.com/ScaryPlaces

Index

About the Author

Joyce Markovics is a children's book author who lives in a 160-year-old house. Chances are that a few otherworldly beings live there, too. Her home is very close to spooky Sleepy Hollow, New York, and the historic—and most definitely haunted—Sing Sing Prison.